P. B. GOLDEN

The People نوكردة

LISSE
THE PETER DE RIDDER PRESS
1976

ISBN 90 316 0048 2

The text of this article is reprinted from
ARCHIVUM EURASIAE MEDII AEVI
I (1975), pp. 21-35

Printed in Belgium

The observation that the reconstruction of the early history and migrations of the tribes that came to form the Hungarians of the 'conquest period' (*honfoglalás*) is a process strewn with many pitfalls has long been a commonplace in Proto-Hungarological studies. Paramount amongst these pitfalls have been the numerous philological problems that arise in connection with the works of the Muslim geographers and historians of the 9th-11th centuries. The difficulties of sifting through these multi-tiered accounts which, for the most part, have come down to us via later compilers and have, in addition, been subjected to the vicissitudes of the copyist's hand, are well-known. Recently, an attempt has been made to place the entire body of Muslim historico-geographical knowledge relating to the Eurasian steppe zone and East-Central Europe into a mosaic of coherent themes.[1]

The focus of our investigation will consist of several passages found in Arab sources relating to the late 9th-early 10th century in which the Proto-Hungarian tribal union (or unions) figures prominently. These passages are not strangers to those who have attempted to unravel various historical knots of this period. Nevertheless, some aspects of these accounts have never been satisfactorily explained.

I

Al-Mas'ûdî (died c. 956-957), the well-known polyhistor and world-traveller, the bulk of whose works have not, apparently, survived,[2] in a

[1] *See* B. N. Zaxoder, *Kaspiiskii svod svedenii o vostočnoi evrope*, Moskva, 1962-1967, i-ii.

[2] C. Brockelmann, *Geschichte der arabischen Litteratur*, Berlin, 1898-1902, Leiden, 1937-1949, i, pp. 143-144; R. A. Nicholson, *A Literary History of the Arabs*, Cambridge Paperback edition, 1969, pp. 352-353; S. M. Ziauddin Alavi, *Arab Geography in the Ninth and Tenth Centuries*, Aligarh, 1965, pp. 31-33. *See* also Marquart's

general statement in his *Murûj adh-Dhahab*, gave a brief account of the activities of a number of nomadic tribes in the Pontic steppe zone : [3]

فلنرجع الآن إلى ما كنا فيه آنفاً من ذكر الأمم المحيطة بالباب والأبواب
والسور وجبل القَبخ وبلاد الخزر واللان؛ فنقول إنه يلي بلاد الخزر واللان
فيما بينهم وبين المغرب أمم اربع تُرك ترجع إلى أب واحد فى بدء أنسابها،
بدو وحضر وذوو منعة وبأسر شديد، لكلّ أمّة منها مَلِك مسافة كلّ مملكة
منها أيام متصّلة ممالكهم بعضها ببحر بنطسر؛ وتتصل غاراتهم ببلاد
رومية ومايلى بلاد الأندلس مستظهرة على سائر مَن هنالك من الأمم؛
وبينهم وبين مَلِك لخزر مهادنة وكذلك مع صاحب اللاَّن، وديارهم تتصل
ببلاد الخزر؛ فالجيل الاوّل منهم يقال له بجَنْىَ ؛[1] ثم يليه أمة ثانية يقال
لها بجَغْرِد؛ ثم يليها أمُةّ يقال لها بَجْناك وهي أشد هذه الامم بأساً؛ تليها
أمة أخرى يقال لها نوكردة [2] وملوكهم بدو

[1] Var. Lect. : يجنى
[2] Var. Lect. : بوكبردة

Let us return now to what we were just discussing with regard to the peoples surrounding Bâb al-Abwâb, the Wall, the Caucasus, the Land of the Xazars and the Alans. We commented that near the Land of the Xazars and the Alans, towards the West, are four Turkic peoples which stem from one father with regard to their origin and kinship. They are nomadic and sedentary. They are difficult of approach and possess great courage. Each of these peoples has a king. Each of their countries is several days in extent. Parts of their countries touch on the Pontus Sea. Their raids reach the Land of Rome and the region near al-Andalus and have gained them victory over the other peoples of these parts. There is a truce between them and the King of the Xazars and also with the Ruler of the Alans. Their region borders on the Land of the Xazars. The first tribe is called بجنى. Near them is the second people who are called بجغرد and near them is a people بجناك; they are the most courageous of these peoples. Near them is the last of these peoples, the نوكردة. Their kings are nomadic.

---

perhaps overly sharp comments: J. Marquart, *Osteuropäische und Ostasiatische Streifzüge*, Leipzig, 1902, reprint : Hildesheim, 1961, pp. XXXIV-XXXV.

[3] Al-Mas'ûdî, *Murûj adh-Dhahab wa Ma'âdin al-Jawhar*, ed. C. Pellat, Beirut, 1966-1970, i, pp. 235-236.

In his *Kitâb at-Tanbîh*, al-Mas'ûdî sheds further light on the situation with regard to these nomadic tribes in the westernmost part of the Pontic steppe zone. Here, he associates them with the town of ولندر and notes : [4]

وقد غلبت البرغر واجناس من الترك بدّو يسمّون الولندريّة اضافة الى مدينة فى اقاصى ثغور الروم مما يلى المشرق تعرف بولندر وهم بجناك ويجنى [1] وبجغرد [2] ونوكبردة [3] على اكثر هذه البنود الخمسة وذلك بعد العشرين والثلاثمائة وخيّموا هناك ومنعوا الطريق من القسطنطينيّة الى رومية وهو مسافة نحو اربعين يوما واخربوا اكثر ما هناك من العمائر واتّصلت غاراتهم بالقسطنطينيّة فلا وصول لمن فى القسطنطينيّة الى رومية فى هذا الوقت الاّ في البحر وانّما العمارة بينهما مما يلى القسطنطينيّة مسيرة ايّام كثيرة وقد ذكرنا في كتاب فنون المعارف وما جرى في الدهور السوالف السبب في انتقال هذه الاجناس الاربعة من الترك عن المشرق وما كان بينهم وبين الغزيّة والخرلخيّه والكيماكيّة من الحروب والغارات على البحيرة الجرجانيّه

[1] Var. Lect. : بجنى* = ويحنى

[2] Var. Lect. : بحرم

[3] Var. Lect. : نوكردة* = ونوكرده ,وبوكرده

The Burğar and tribes of nomadic Turks, who are called الولندريّة after a town located at the extremes of the border of Rûm (Byzantium), towards the East, which is known as ولندر (these nomadic Turks) are the بجناك the *بجنى, the بجغرد and the نوكردة, conquered most of these five provinces. This was after the year 320/932. They camp here and block the road from Constantinople to Rome. This is a distance of some forty days journey. They have ravaged most of the land under cultivation there and their raids reach Constantinople and no one can go from Constantinople to Rome at this time except by sea; for the land under cultivation between the two of them is a distance of many days. We have mentioned in (our) "Book of the Science of What Happened in Ages Past" (*Kitâb Funûn al-Ma'ârif wa Mâ Jarâ fî'd-Duhûr as-Sawâlif*) the reason for the movement of the Turks from the East and what occured between them and the *Oğuz, *Qarluq and Kimäk, of the wars and raids around the Sea of Jurjân.

[4] Al-Mas'ûdî, *Kitâb at-Tanbîh wa'l-Ischrâf*, ed. M. J. de Goeje, Leiden, 1894, pp. 180-181.

A confirmation of this latter notice is found in an abbreviated form in the later chronicle of Ibn al-Athîr (d. 1234). The latter notes :[5]

وممّا ينبغي أن يلحق بهذا أن الطوائف من الترك اجتمعت، منهم البجناك والبختى [1] وغيرها، وقصدوا مدينة للروم قديمة تسمّى وليدر [2] سنة اثنتين وعشرين وثلاثمائة وحصروها، فبلغ خبرهم إلى أرمانوس، فسيّر إليهم عسكراً كثيفاً فيهم من المتنصّرة اثنا عشر ألفاً، فاقتتلوا قتالاً شديداً، فانهزم الرومُ، واستولى الترك على المدينة وخرّبوها بعد أن أكثروا القتل فيها والسبي والنهب، ثمّ ساروا إلى القسطنطينيّة وحصروها أربعين يوماً وأغاروا على بلاد الروم واتصّلت غاراتهم إلى بلاد الإفرنج، ثمّ عادوا راجعين

[1] البختى = البجنى*

[2] Var. Lect. ولتدر and the correct ولندر

It seems to me that in this (year), tribes of the Turks came together and formed a union; these were the بجناك and بختى (=بجنى*) and two others. They moved against and old city of Rûm called وليدر (=ولندر) in the year 322/933-934 and besieged it. News of them came to Ârmânûs (Romanus Lecapenus, Byzantine Emperor 920-944) and he went out against them with a large army of Christians, 12,000 in number. They fought a ferocious battle and the Rûm were defeated. The Turks took possession of the city and destroyed it after having increased in it the (number of) killed, captive and pillaged. Then, they marched on Constantinople and besieged it for forty days and they raided the land of Rûm and their raids reached the land of the Franks. Then, they returned home.

II

1. Marquart, in his *Streifzüge*, made a detailed analysis of these notices.[6] He noted that this was a period of intensive raiding on the part of the Hungarians and briefly catalogued a number of raids in Germany, Italy, Byzantium, and France (including points close to Muslim Spain)

[5] Ibn al-Athîr, *Al-Kâmil fî't-t-Ta'rîx* : *Chronicon quod perfectissimum inscribitur*, ed. C. J. Tornberg (Leiden, 1851-1876, Beirut reprint, 1965-1966—the pagination of the latter differs somewhat from the Leiden edition. I have used the Beirut edition), i, p. 339.

[6] Marquart, *Streifzüge*, pp. 61-68.

in the 920s through the 940s.[7] He then concluded that the Hungarians were included amongst the Turkic tribes of ولندر. In a later article, Marquart indicated that ولندر (*Wulundur* in his reading) is to be derived from the tribal name *Onoğundur* and suggested the following comparisons : *Οὐνογουνδοῦροι* (Nicephorus), الغندر Uluğundur (Ibn al-Kalbî), *Olxontor* (Ananias Širakec'i) > *W(u)ł(u)ndur Bulkar* (Ps. Movsês Xorenac'i), *Wunundur* (*Ḥudûd al-ʿÂlam*), ولندر *Wulundur* (al-Masʿûdî) = Hung. Nándor Fejérvár = Belgrad.[8] To this grouping we might also add the ונתר (*W n nt r*) of the Qazar Hebrew Correspondence and the نندر (*N nd r*) of Gardîzî.[9] Marquart's suggestions would place the geographical setting of our notices in the North-eastern Balkans. Ibn Rusta, in a notice discussed below (IV.2 — a notice that caused Marquart some trouble) confirms this.

2. Our main concern is the identification of the nomads mentioned in these notices. The بجناك (Bajanâk = *Päčänā̄k, *cf.* Rus' : Печенѣг) are, of course, the Pečenegs, who were driven, as al-Masʿûdî noted, from their original homelands in the Syr Daryâ region (K'ang-kü of the Chinese sources) into the trans-Volga steppe zone and thence into the Pontic steppes. The form, as we have it here, is very common in Islamic sources.[10] The بجغرد are, undoubtedly, the Proto-Hungarians

[7] A useful outline of the raids can be seen in the map given in J. Deér, "A honfoglaló magyarság" in L. Ligeti (ed.), *A magyarság őstörténete* (henceforward abbreviated as *Mőt*—Budapest, 1943), p. 133. On the Hungarian raids *see* also : R. Lüttich, *Ungarnzüge in Europa im 10. Jahrhundert* (Berlin, 1910), esp. chap. IV; Gy. Pauler, *A magyar nemzet története Szent Istvánig* (henceforward abbreviated as *MNT*—Budapest, 1900), chaps. V-IX; B. Hóman, Gy. Szekfü, *Magyar történet* (Budapest, 1935²), esp. i, pp. 139-142; G. Fasoli, *Le incursioni ungare in Europa nel secolo X* (Florence, 1945).

[8] J. Marquart, "Ein arabischer Bericht über die arktischen (uralischen) Länder aus dem 10. Jahrhundert", *Ungarische Jahrbücher* 4 (1924), p. 275.

[9] P. K. Kokovtsov, *Evreisko–xazarskaia perepiska v X veke*, Leningrad, 1932, pp. 28 (Hebrew text), p. 92 (trans.); Gardîzî in : *A magyar honfoglalás kútfői*, eds. Gy. Pauler, S. Szilágy, Budapest, 1900, pp. 169 ff.; V. V. Bartol'd (Barthold), "Otčët o poezdke v sredniuiu aziiu s naučnoi tsel'iu v 1893-1894 g.", *Zapiski Imperatorskoi Akademii Nauk*, VIII, seriia po istoriko-filologičeskomu otdeleniiu, i, No. 4 (1897), pp. 98 (text), pp. 121-122 (trans.).

[10] *Cf.* the forms بجناك, بجاناكية in : Ibn Rusta, *Kitâb al-A'lâķ an-Nafîsa*, ed. M. J. de Goeje, Leiden, 1982, pp. 139 *passim*; Ibn Faḍlân : A. Z. V. Toğan, *Ibn Faḍlân's Reisebericht* in *Abhandlungen für die Kunde des Morgenlandes*, 24 iii (1939), pp. 17 ff. (Arabic text); Al-Iṣṭaxrî, *Kitâb Masâlik al-Mamâlik*, ed. M. J. de Goeje, Leiden, 1870, p. 10 *passim*, Ibn Ḥawqal, *Kitâb Surat al-Arḍ*, ed. J. H. Kramers, Leiden–Leipzig, 1938-1939, ii, p. 15 *passim*, A. Kunik, V. Rozen, *Izvestiia al-Bekri i drugix avtorov o rusi i slavianax*, supplement to the *Zapiski imperatorskoi Akademii Nauk*, 32 ii, čast' pervaia (1878), pp. 42 ff. On the Pečeneg migrations, *see* P. Golden, "The Migrations of the Oğuz", *Archivum Ottomanicum* 4 (1972).

or elements of them. Islamic sources frequently use the ethnonym بجغرد for them.[11] This much was clear to Marquart. Similarly, he saw no difficulty in identifying *بجنى (*Pačnâ) as "nur eine Nebenform für بجناك".[12] It is with نوكردة, then, that our serious difficulties begin.

Géza Kuun long ago suggested that نوكردة was a corruption of *nöker-ler* (Turkic plural of *nöker*, a Mongol loanword in Turkic) 'milites' and compared it with Mong. *nökür* (and from Mong., Čağ. *nöker* etc.) 'socius, amicus, servus' noting, then, "idem esse videtur quod vocabulum turcicum scriptor Arabus falso pro nomine ethnico alicujus tribuum turcicarum habuit".[13]

Gyula Pauler, continuing the thesis that نوكردة must be a corruption of some other form badly garbled in the Arab sources, suggested that, since بجنى and بجناك refer to one and the same people, بجغرد and نوكردة must go together. *Nökerdeh* (in his transcription) was clearly, in his view, a corruption of *Meger–Magyar*.[14] The philological obstacles that one would have to surmount to arrive at this conclusion were never explained.

Marquart also saw in نوكردة a corruption of some other form. He first noted the difficulties encountered in understanding the text on the basis of the forms as given. (The editor of al-Mas'ûdî's *Kitâb at-Tanbîh*, M. J. de Goeje, viewed it as a garbling of *Langobard*. As can be seen from the Arabic form of this name, الأَنْكَبَرْدَة, الانكبرديين, it is graphically very close to نوكردة.) Marquart commented: "Wenn

[11] See V. V. Bartol'd, "Basjirt", *Sočineniia* (Moskva, 1968), v, pp. 494-495. On the broader question of the Magyar–Baškir connection, *see* Pauler, *MNT*, pp. 241-264; Gy. Németh, *A honfoglaló magyarság kialakulása* (henceforward abbreviated as *HMK* — Budapest, 1930), pp. 299-315; K. Czeglédy, "Keleten maradt magyar töredékek", *MŐt*, pp. 154-177; L. Rásonyi, *Tarihte Türklük*, Ankara, 1971, pp. 123-125. Rudenko (S. I. Rudenko, *Baškiry. Istoriko-ètnografičeskie očerki*, Moskva–Leningrad, 1955, esp. pp. 342-343, and 351) notes Ugric elements amongst the present-day Baškirs.

[12] Marquart, *Streifzüge*, p. 67. This form of the name is also found in Oğuz legend, *cf.* the بجنه of the *Šäjärä-i Tärâkimä* (*Rodoslovnaia Turkmen*, ed. trans. A. N. Kononov, Moskva–Leningrad, 1958, lines 521, 557, 606, 704, 706, 707 and 1255).

The forms يجنى *Yajnâ/Yagnâ and بختى *Baxtî etc. must be viewed as corruptions of بجنى via a change in dotting (a phenomonen very common in Arabic script manuscripts) as we possess no other notices indicating the existence of tribes with these names.

[13] G. Kuun, *Relationum Hungarorum cum oriente gentibusque orientalis originis historia antiquissima*, Claudiopoli, MDCCCXCI, pp. 73-75. On the word *nökür*, *see*: Gy. Németh, "Wanderungen des Mongolischen Wortes *nökür* 'Genosse'" *Acta Orientalia Hungarica* 3 (1953).

[14] Pauler, *MNT*, p. 142.

man die نُوكَرْدَة in نوكبردة [15] ändert und für Langobarden erklärt, wie de Goeje in seiner Ausgabe des Kitâb attanbîh thut, so vergrössert sich nur die Schwierigkeit. Denn was haben die Langobarden mit den Pečenegen und Magyaren zu thun, ausser dass sie gleich den Deutschen von den Einfällen der letzteren heimgesucht wurden?" [16]

Marquart proposed that نوكردة was a corruption of *بزكردة (*Bazgarda*) or *بژكردة (*Bažgarda*) and concluded that بژكردة and پچنا were simply "neupersischischen Formen für älteres بجكرد und پچناك".[17]

Minorsky, in his commentary to the *Ḥudûd al-ʿÂlam*, remarked, in passing, that "Nukarda" was still "obscure".[18] In his later study of the part of the Münejjimbašı chronicle dealing with the Caucasus, he suggested, following Frähn and Charmoy, that نوكردة = **Naugarda* 'Novgorodians', 'perhaps *Novgorodian adventurers (*brodniki*) living among the Turkish nomads'.[19] Still further afield was the speculation of S. P. Tolstov that the "zagadočnyi narod Naukerde" were somehow to be associated with Yangıkänt (*Naukat*).[20]

The solutions proposed by C. A. Macartney were much closer to the mark. Nonetheless, he left a number of philological problems unresolved. Following the *ʿAjâ'ib ad-Dunyâ* (ascribed to al-Masʿûdî) and ad-Dimašqî, he contended that نوكردة should be compared with the اهتردة of the *ʿAjâ'ib ad-Dunyâ* and the انكردة of ad-Dimašqî.[21] In the latter's *Nuxbat ad-Dahr*, the الانكردة (**al-Unkarda, al-Ungarda*) are noted as neighbors of the افرنج (*Ifranj, i.e.* 'the Franks' Latin Christendom). The editor of the text, Mehrens, mistakenly read the name as a corruption of الانكبردة, *i.e.* the Langobards.[22] Elsewhere, ad-Dimašqî,

[15] Marquart is here refering to the comparison with the * الانكبرديين (so de Goeje) of Ibn Rusta to which we shall return, *see* below.

[16] Marquart, *Streifzüge*, pp. 66-67. For the form الانكبردة, *see* Yâqût, *Muʿjam al-Buldân*, Beirut, no date, i, p. 262 under the entry : الاندلس.

[17] Marquart, *Streifzüge*, p. 67.

[18] *Ḥudûd al-ʿÂlam*, trans. V. Minorsky, London, 1937, reprint, 1970, p. 466 of the commentary.

[19] V. Minorsky, *A History of Sharvân and Darband*, Cambridge, 1958, pp. 113, 160 n. 2.

[20] S. P. Tolstov, *Po sledam drevnexorezmiiskoi tsivilizatsii*, Moskva–Leningrad, 1948, p. 246.

[21] C. A. Macartney, *The Magyars in the Ninth Century*, Cambridge, 1930, pp. 23 n. 4, 34 n. 3, and 152; *idem*, "The Attack on Valandar", *Byzantinisch-Neugriechische Jahrbücher* 8 (1931), pp. 159-162.

[22] Al-Dimašqî : Ed-Dimichqui, *Nukhbat ad-Dahr fî ʿAdschâ'ib al-Barr wa'l Bahr*, ed. A. Mehren, St. Peterburg, 1866, reprint : Leipzig, 1918, p. 207.

in a notice on the peoples of the Black Sea (بحرالروس 'Sea of the Rûs in his terminology), cites the following peoples : الروس, أركش, ألآن, الهنكر (!), باشقرد, and القبجاق. This is an obvious amalgam of notices (given the presence of the اركش [23]) drawn from a variety of sources. Significantly, however, the هنكر (*Hunkar*, *Hungar*) and باشقرد (*Bâš-qurd*) have been placed side by side.[24] The detailed notice on the اهتردة in the *'Ajâ'ib ad-Dunyâ*, reads as follows :

ذكر الاهتردة

وأمّا الاهتردة فهم من ولد عامر بن يافث نزلوا بين الروم والافرنج ومملكتهم واسعة، وملكهم جليل القدر ولهم مدن كثيرة وأكثرهم اليوم نصارى، ومنهم لادين له وهم يحاربون الافرنج والصقالبة الذين يجاورونهم ويطردونهم، وزيهم زي الروم، ومنهم صنف يحرقون أنفسهم ...[25]

Notice on the اهتردة. As concerns the اهتردة, they are descendants of 'Âmir son of Yâfath. They have settled between Rûm and the Franks (Latino-Germanic West). Their kingdom is vaste. Their king possesses great power. At present, the bulk of them are Christians. There are those amongst them who do not follow any faith. They war with the Franks and the Ṣaqâliba (Slavs) who neighbor on them and drive them away. Their dress is that of Rûm. There are those amongst them who burn themselves.

Macartney, on the basis of the contents of this notice and the variant reading *al-Ankiradah* (taken from the translation *L'Abrégé des Merveilles*, trans. M. Carra de Vaux, Paris, 1898, inaccessible to me; the recent Arabic edition of this work does not note a variant reading), deduced that the اهتردة must be the Hungarians.

[23] For the آركش/أذكش a tribe appearing in a listing of tribes in the 9th century, *see* Ibn Xurdâdhbih, *Kitâb al-Masâlik wa'l-Mamâlik*, ed. M. J. de Goeje, Leiden, 1889, p. 31 and Ibn al-Faqîh (*Kitâb al-Buldân*, ed. M. J. de Goeje, Leiden, 1885, p. 329) who follows him.

[24] Similarly, Abû'l-Fidâ (*Géographie d'Aboulféda*, ed. M. Reinaud and M. Bon MacGuckin de Slane, Paris, 1840, p. 206) places the باشقرد, who border on the الامانيين (*al-Âmânîyyun* 'Germans') and who were converted to Islam by some Turkmän *faqîh*, west of the بلاد الهنقر ('land of the Hunqar'), "the brothers of the Bâšqurd who have become Christians, because of their proximity to the Germans". Abû'l-Fidâ (d. 1331) evidently confused the Baškir (in Baškir : *Bašqort*) of Baškiria with the historical memory of the Bašqırd (Bajğird etc.)–Hungarian relationship.

[25] Al-Mas'ûdî, *Axbar az-Zamân wa min Âbâdihi'l-Ḥidthân wa 'Ajâ'ib al-Buldân wa Ğâmir bi'l-Mâ' wa'l-'Umrân*, Beirut, 1966, p. 96.

There is little doubt that the انكردة are, indeed, the Hungarians. اهتردة is, most probably, a garbling of this form (perhaps contaminated with هنكر). The * انكرديين of Ibn Rusta (*see* below) and the بلاد انكريد (*بلاد انكرية) of al-Idrîsî [26] are obviously *bona fide* variants. The exact philological relationship between انكردة/اهتردة and نوكردة which Macartney postulates, however, was never explained.

3. نوكردة is not simply a corrupted form of انكردة. For this to be so, a very considerable emendation of our texts would be required. We would be forced to create a form *اونكردة for which no textual justification exists. The transposition of نو to read ون (producing *ونكردة) which Macartney implies, while appearing a simple emendation in the Latin alphabet, radically changes the word in its Arabic garb. Such a form, **Wungarda*, remains unattested in our sources and, although explanations can be conjured up for it, these would, perforce, be labored. Equally important, Macartney is not forthcoming with any explanation of the دة ending in the forms نوكردة, انكردة etc.

III

1. هنقر and هنكر clearly reflect *Hungar*, the name by which the Hungarians were and are called today by their neighbors (Ungar, Węgier, Venger, *Οὔγγρος*, etc.). This name, as was long ago established, derives from *Onoğur*, the name of an Oğuric Turkic tribal union with which elements of the tribes that formed the Hungarian tribal union of the 'conquest period' were closely associated.[27] The forms نوكردة and انكردة are variants of this name. نوكردة should be read as **Nogurda* = *Onogurda* (انكردة may be *Ungarda* or *Ungurda*). The loss of an initial vowel in the transcription of foreign words, especially Turkic (or Turko-

[26] Al-Idrîsî : T. Lewicki, *Polska i kraje sąsiednie w świetle "księgi Rogera" geografa arabskiego z XII w. al-Idrîsî'ego*, Warszawa, 1954, ii, p. 31; *Géographie d'Édrisi*, trans. P. A. Jaubert in *Recueil de Voyages et de Mémoires*, 5 i-ii (Paris, 1836-1840), ii, p. 375.

[27] *See* Gy. Moravcsik, "Zur Geschichte der Onoguren", *Ungarische Jahrbücher* 10 (1930), pp. 53-90 (now reprinted in Gy. Moravcsik, *Studia Byzantina*, Amsterdam, 1967, pp. 84-118); Németh, *HMK*, pp. 178-182; E. Moór, "Die Benennungen der Ungarn in den Quellen des IX. und X. Jahrhunderts" *Ural-Altaische Jahrbücher*, 31 (1959), pp. 215-225. On the Ottoman انكروس (< Lat. *Hungarus*), *see* T. Halasi-Kun, "Avrupa'daki Osmanlı yer adları üzerinde araştırmalar, *Peşte*, انكروس", *Türk Dili ve Tarihi Hakkında Araştırmalar* 1 (1950), pp. 97-104.

Hungarian) in Arabic (Greek, Latin, Slavic, and other languages as well) is not uncommon. Thus, as Marquart noted (*see* above), *Onoğundur*, a variant of *Onoğur*, became *Vunundur* (with the prothetic *v* typical of Oğuric) and finally نندر *N nd r* in Gardîzî. The well-known ethnonym *Oğuz* is regularly rendered in Islamic sources as غز *Ğuzz*. In modern Syrian Arabic dialects (where loss of initial *i* is common), the Western European (via Ottoman) loan-word *İspanya* ('Spain') becomes *Şbânya.*[28] The Bulgarian prince, *Omurtag*, appears in Byzantine sources as both *'Ομουρτάγ* and *Μορταγων*. The Hungaro-Slavic hydronym *Laborc* (< **Labars*) stems from Turkic *Alp Bars.*[29]

2. The دة ending, completely overlooked in previous discussions of نوكردة, انكردة, is the Hungarian diminutive-affectionate ending : *-d*, *-da*, *-di*, *-dü* etc. At this time, these forms were widely used. The most prominent example of this is the name of the Proto-Hungarian tribal grouping mentioned by Constantine Prophyrogenitus and Eastern sources : *Σάβαρτοι ἄσφαλοι* [30] (= *Savardi* < *Sabır*, *Sabar*). Other examples of tribal names in this form (often appearing as personal or place names) are *Zuard* ('Savard'), *Besenyőd* (< *Besenyő* 'Pečeneg'), *Uzd* ('Oğuz', 'Uz' '*Οὖζοι*'), *Mogurdi* (< 'Magyar'), *Kozárd* (< 'Qazar'), etc.[31]

IV. THE * انكردين OF IBN RUSTA

1. On the basis of the above, it is fitting that we now turn to the passage of Ibn Rusta regarding the * انكردين. Marquart wrestled with it in his *Streifzüge* and (as was not atypical of him) reversed his views in the course of the work.[32] Again it is useful to to see the passage in full. It is part of a longer notice on the Balkans :

[28] T. Halasi-Kun, "The Ottoman Elements in the Syrian Dialects", *Archivum Ottomanicum* 1 (1969), p. 56.

[29] Gy. Moravcsik, *Byzantinoturcica*, Berlin, 1958, ii, pp. 217-218; I. Kniezsa, *Magyarország népei a XI. században*, Budapest, 1938, p. 436 n. 1.

[30] Constantinus Porphyrogenitus, *De Administrando Imperio*, ed. trans. Gy. Moravcsik–R. Jenkins in *Corpus Fontium Historiae Byzantinae*, i (Washington, D. C., 1967), p. 170.

[31] Németh, *HMK*, pp. 169-170, 193, and 318. *Cf.* also *Besenyődi* (Kniezsa, *Magyarország népei*, p. 471).

[32] Marquart, *Streifzüge*, pp, 66 n. 2, 237-243. The text in question is Ibn Rusta, ed. de Goeje, pp. 127-128.

... سلوقية [1] وهى مدينة عظيمة كبيرة مما يلى مشرق المدينة الجبل وغربيّها البحر ولها اربعة انهار تسقيها وفيها دير يقال له مرقش فيه اثنا عشر الف راهب وتخرج فتسير على ساحل البحر ثلاث منازل في صحراء ليس فيها من العمران شئٌ وهى مدينة عظيمة فيها اسواق وحواليها انهار كثيرة وتسقيها انهار مُطرن وعليها سوران وخندق يحيط بالمدينة، وتخرج منها فتسير في غياض من الشجر في وسط الصقالبة لهم بيوت من خشب ينزلونها وهم نصارى كانوا يتنصَّرون على عهد بسوس الملك فهم اليوم على دين النصرانيَّة فتسير فيهم مقدار شهر فى مشاجرهم حتّى تنتهى الى مدينة يقال لها بلاطيس [2] وهى مدينة عظيمة طولها ستّة اميال في مثلها وهى كثيرة الخير فيها من الزيتون وانواع الفواكه ولها نهران جاريان يطّردان فيها وهى مدينة الانكُبرْدِيّين [3] قد نزلوا في صحاريهم على مقدار عشرين خطوةً وهم على هيئة الاكراد ينزلون الصحارى في الخيام وتخرج من هذه القرية فتسير وسطهم مقدار شهر فى غياض واشابحار وربَّما يلقاك تلال فيها منهم اصناف حُلول حتّى تنتهى الى قرية تدعى البندقيس وهم نزول في صحراء ملساء ليس لهم

[1] = *سلونيقية

[2] de Goeje: "Fortasse corruptum e nomine تيتلوس Τιτέλιος.

[3] Cod. الانكبودينى.

... S lûqîyya (Salonika). It is a large and great town. To the east of the town is a mountain and in the west is the sea. It has four rivers which water it. In it is a monastery called *M r q š* (for مرقس Marcus?) in which (live) 12,000 monks. One goes out and journeys along the seashore for three days through plains. Nothing is under cultivation there. It is a great town with markets in it and great rivers pass it. The rivers of مطرن (Marquart, *Streifzüge*, pp. 237-238, suggests قطرن *Qutron, *cf.* *Κίτρος*) water it. It has a double wall and a moat surrounds the town. One goes out from it and travels in forests in the heart of the Ṣaqâliba land. They have houses of wood in which they live. They are Christians. They have become Christians in the time of بسوس [for *بوريس Boris, the Bulgar Xan who converted in 864, or *بسيل *i.e. βασίλειος*, either a generic term for the Byzantine Emperor or Basil I (867-886), who played a role in the extension of Byzantine power and Orthodox Christianity to Serbia (*see* A. P. Vlasto, *The Entry of the Slavs into Christendom*, Cambridge, 1970, pp. 207-208, and F. Dvornik, *Byzantine Missions Among the Slavs*, New Bruns-

wick, 1970, pp. 37-38). The text is uncelear as to which Slavs were converted.], the king. And they are today of the Christian faith. One travels amongst them for a number of months through forests until one reaches the town called بلاطيس. It is a great town, approximately six square miles in length. It has many goods, such as olives and various fruits. It has two rivers which flow and cross one another in it. This is the city of the *انكرديين. They have settled in its plains to an extent of twenty *خطوة. They live like Kurds, in tents in the plains. One leaves this village and travels through them for one month, through thickets and forests and occasionally one encounters a hillock in which are various settlements of them, until one ends up at a village called البندقيس....

2. The الانكبرديين of the Goeje edition of Ibn Rusta (the manuscript has (الانكبوديني) is a corruption of الانكردية via a confusion with الانكبردية, as has already been suggested. It is obvious from the text that we are dealing with the still nomadic Hungarians ('They live like Kurds, in tents in the plains') relatively newly arrived in the region. This could not possibly be the Langobards (Lombards) who were pushed out of this area in the 6th century by the Avars.[33] بلاطيس of our text should be restored to *تلاطيس, a garbling of *تطاليس Tiṭâlîs = Byz. *Τιτέλιος*, Hung. *Titel*, which al-Idrîsî (in the form تيتلوس) noted as belonging to the country of the انكريه.[34] Titel is in Bács county. Prior to the Hungarian conquest, it was ruled by a certain *Salanus*, whose political center it was. He was probably under the overlordship of the Danubian Bulgars and ruled over a predominantly Slavic population. The toponyms of the region indicate that elements of the Nyék, Megyer, Kürt, Gyarmat, Tarján, Kér, and Keszi tribes of the Hungarian tribal union were in this area. Hungarian hegemony was extended to this region in the 10th century under the Árpádids Zolta and Szerénd.[35] It is easy to see, given the graphic similarities of الانكردة etc. and الانكبردة and the historical memory of the Langobards as the onetime masters of this region, from whence the confusion of these forms derives.

[33] A. Kollautz – H. Miyakawa, *Geschichte und Kultur eines völkerwanderungszeitlichen Nomadenvolkes*, Klagenfurt, 1970, i, pp. 168-170. Constantine Porphyrogenitus (*DAI*, ed. Moravcsik – Jenkins, p. 114) notes that the Hungarians (*Τοῦρκοι*) in his day lived in Pannonia where the Langobards (*Λαγούβαρδοι*) once lived.

[34] Al-Idrîsî: Géographie d'Édrisi, trans. Jaubert, ii, p. 378; Lewicki, *Polska i kraje sąsiednie*, ii, p. 67.

[35] Gy. Györffy, *Az Árpád-kori magyarország történeti földrajza*, Budapest, 1963, pp. 201-202, and 240-242. Marquart's emendations (*see* the *Streifzüge*, pp. 237-243), in light of this, must be rejected.

V. بجغرد AND نوكردة

As we indicated in our introductory remarks, there are still many unresolved questions in Hungarian protohistory. Our texts (which, for the most part, relate to the first third of the 10th century), unfortunately, still do not provide definitive solutions to some of the major questions of this complex subject that have recently been raised. To gain some perspective, it will be useful to review, in a greatly abbreviated fashion, the two major reconstructions of the origins of the "Conquest Period Hungarians". The classic outline of Hungarian protohistory was sketched by Németh, in great detail and with a wealth of information regarding the patterns of steppe history as a whole.[36] In a recent article, which emended some of his earlier conclusions, Németh proposed that the Hungarian tribal union was originally located in what is today Baškiria. There, they were in a symbiosis with the Oğuric Volga–Kama Bulgars. They migrated from this area c. 750-800 to the Lower Don–Volga–North Caucasus triangle and settled near the Sea of Azov (Maeotis). Here, under Qazar overlordship, they were known, in Hungarian tradition, as the *Dentü Mogyer* ('Magyars of the Don').[37] In this region, they once again came under Oğuric (Bulgaric) influences from remnants of the old Onoğur tribal union (also under Qazar rule). The name *Onoğur*, just as *Sabir* and *Türk*, became associated with them, giving rise to *Ungar*, *Hungar*, *Οὔγγροι*, etc.[38] They were driven from this region by the Pečenegs and forced ultimately into Pannonia, their present homeland.

Recently, this view was challenged on some very fundamental points by I. Boba, who presented the case for the existence of two separate and distinct tribal unions, the *Magyar* (*Majğar*) and *Onoğur*, who joined together only at the end of the 9th century to form the Hungarians of the "Conquest Period".[39]

[36] Németh, *HMK*, esp. pp. 8-84 on the system of tribal-names and name-giving in the nomadic Turkic world.

[37] *Cf.* the "Turk" city داني of Ibn al-Faqîh (T. Lewicki, *Źródła arabskie do dziejów słowiańszczyzny.* (Wrocław–Warszawa–Kraków, 1969), ii/1, p. 42 (Arab text), p. 126 (commentary)—this passage taken from the Mašhad manuscript is not found in the de Goeje edition which appeared before the discovery of the Mašhad manuscript). *See* also Lewicki's article "Türkische Stadt Dânâ—nach einem Bericht des Arabischen Geographen Ibn al-Faqîh", *Folia Orientalia* 13 (1971), pp. 161-170.

[38] Gy. Németh, "A Baskír földi magyar őshazáról", *Élet és Tudomány* 13 (1966). On the historical circumstances that brought about the Hungarian migrations, *see* Golden, "The Migrations of the Oğuz", *Archivum Ottomanicum* 4 (1972).

[39] *See* : I. Boba, *Nomads, Northmen and Slaves* (The Hague–Wiesbaden, 1967).

Given the overall *schemata* traced above, what are we to conclude regarding the بجغرد and نوكردة of our texts? As is not infrequent in steppe history, where sources are scarce and speculation abundant, a number of *potential* solutions present themselves. Bits and pieces found elsewhere in our sources do not aid us. Thus, al-Mas'ûdî, in another notice in the *Murûj*,[40] under the heading "Notice on the Sea of Bunṭus (Pontus), the Sea of Mâyuṭis and the Straits of Constantinople" states :

البرغر والروس وبَجْنَى وبجْناك وبَجغِرْد وهم ثلاثة أنواع من الترك

The Burğar, the Rûs, the *Päcänā̈, the Päčänāk and the Bajğird, (the latter) are three tribes of the Turk...

This would appear to make the Pečeneg and Pečene distinct from one another. More important is the absence of the نوكردة. Were they subsumed by the Bajğird? Are they not yet on the scene? Or, as is most likely in the view of this writer, has al-Mas'ûdî, in attempting to make sense out of the various accounts, written and oral, he had at his disposal, simply omitted the less familiar نوكردة? With regard to our notices in al-Mas'ûdî, we are obliged to state that it is impossible to determine whether we are dealing with one tradition, more or less faithfully preserved, or several accounts which were fused into one, in which material incompatible with al-Mas'ûdî's overall understanding of the situation was edited out. With these caveats in mind, we may offer, in a very tentative way, a number of suggestions whose confirmation will have to await the appearance of new source material.

1. بجغرد, which has been etymologized in a variety of ways (*see* Németh, *HMK*, pp. 309-313; Németh suggests *Bajğird*/*Bašqırd* etc. < **Bäš(o)ğurd*), may be a variant form of (ية) مجغر : *Bajğard*/*Bajğird* (with Hungarian Hungarian *-d* ending) ~ *Majğar*. This might render the 'confusion' of بجغرد and مجغرية [41] in Islamic sources more understandable. *M* ~ *b* alternations in Turkic (many of the informants of our sources were certainly Turks) are very common.

[40] Al-Mas'ûdî, *Murûj*, ed. Pellat, i, pp. 140-141.

[41] Moór ("Die Bennenungen der Ungarn...", *Ural-Altaische Jahrbücher* 31 (1959), p. 227) suggests that Bašğır "aus einer volksetymologischen Aneignung der urungarischen Namensform * moǯ'hər hervorgegangen ist..." A recapitulation of various theories can be found in Rásonyi, *Tarihte Türklük*, p. 125.

Viewed in this light, our sources would appear to have reflected the existence of two tribal unions, the *Majğar/Bajğird* and the نوكردة (the actual Onoğurs?) that came to form the "Hungarians of the Conquest Period".

2. In opposition to this, however, we may note the following:

a) the sequence of tribes, *Pečeneg-Pečene*, *Bajğird-*Onogurda* may just as easily be construed to represent two separate and distinct traditions which were, indeed, misinterpreted and 'spliced together' by al-Mas'ûdî or his source. We would, then, be dealing with only two tribal groupings in the overall picture: the Pečeneg-Pečene and the Proto-Hungarian *Bajğird* ~ *Onogurda*, the latter tribal grouping appearing under different names in the two (or more?) hypothetical traditions.

b) The form نوكردة would appear to be a strong argument in favor of the latter suggestion. It is obviously the Hungarian form of this name. Why would the Onoğurs advertise themselves in Hungarian garb (*cf.* the *-da* ending)? Finally, one may note that the use of ك for rendering *g* is rather more reminiscent of Persian (cf. Ibn Rusta, a Persian writing in Arabic but employing a system of transliteration of foreign names that would appear to reflect Persian rather than Arabic usage: بلكر for بلغار etc.). Are we dealing, then, with two traditions, one Arab (بجغرد, بجناك) and one Persian (بجنى, نوكردة) as the source for al-Mas'ûdî's notice?

FSC
www.fsc.org
MIX
Papier | Fördert
gute Waldnutzung
FSC® C083411

Kolibri 360 GmbH
Ferdinand-Jühlke-Straße 7
99095 Erfurt, Deutschland
produktsicherheit@kolibri360.de